Cooking With Olive Oil

A Guide to Olive Oil

Table of Contents

Cooking With Olive Oil 1

Table of Contents 2

Introduction 3

Chapter 1: The Goodness of Olive Oil 6

Chapter 2: 27 Amazing and Easy Everyday Recipes Using Olive oil 10

Chapter 3: Your Shopping List - Essential Ingredients used in this Book 46

Conclusion 49

Introduction

I want to thank you and congratulate you for purchasing the book *"Cooking With Olive Oil: A Guide to Olive Oil"*.

I am hooked on to cooking with this oil! Why not! Olive oil has been everyone's favorite ingredient for years. It is delicious, versatile and provides a world of health benefits. Olive oil offers unrivaled health benefits and hence is the cornerstone for cuisines across the globe. Everyone who has tried olive oil has fallen in love with it. It is delicious and adds a unique taste to any food you prepare. Olive oil is loaded with antioxidants and is one of the healthiest fats on earth. Olive oil is considered to be super healthy and in most of the countries it definitely is considered as a 'super food'. This book is an attempt to get you closer to the benefits that this oil can provide.

Due to its unique flavor and nourishing nature, olive oil is the perfect choice for almost every kind of cooking. Whether you are baking, sautéing, making salads, soup or a stir-fry, olive oil is versatile and a healthier option in comparison to other oils. This book provides you details on the various health benefits that olive oil can provide and some smart recipes that you can cook with some basic ingredients found in almost every household. Just drizzle a few drops of this golden oil onto your lentil soup, chicken stew, lamb ribs or even your baked chicken. You will be amazed at the appetizing twist it can give to anything you make! Olive oil seems to make anything taste better with its intense flavor and richness.

You will love this book! It is packed with more information than you can ever visualize. It divides 27 lip-smacking recipes into sections as Appetizers, Soups, Salads, Pastas and Rice and Desserts. All these recipes involve different types of olive oil in a creative way. It is a ready guide to enhance your everyday cooking. The recipes shared are easy, the ingredients required can be bought easily and it will not consume much of your time and energy. Most importantly, you will be showered with compliments for the delectable meals you prepare. Now who doesn't want to be praised? This book will inspire you to experiment with different ingredients, most importantly different types of olive oil. The last chapter will give you an easy and quick peek into the essential ingredients that you might have to stock in your kitchen.

I am sure by now you are longing to try the tasty recipes. Not only are you going to indulge palates, you are also on your way to provide a healthy life for all. You are on your way to be the 'master health chef' for your family and friends! So let's cook the 'olive way'!

Chapter 1: The Goodness of Olive Oil

The farming of Olives began nearly 6000 years ago in the Mediterranean region. The people there primarily used it for lighting lamps, cooking as well as in perfumes. Subsequently, olives were cultivated and traded by the Greek, the Moroccans, the Spanish, the Italians and the Romans. As years passed, the use of olive oil in cooking gradually went up because of its unique flavor and goodness.

Today, Spain is the largest producer of the best quality olive oil, followed by Italy, Greece and Turkey. Other countries like Australia, Africa and California also produce olive oil, each possessing an exclusive flavor. Though olive oil is primarily produced in these countries, it is used widely across the world.

This popularity of olive oil is attributed to the distinctive flavor it adds to food and the health benefits it provides. The regional climatic condition, hugely impacts the oil's nature. Usually, the hotter the country of its origin, the more robust flavor the oil has. Olive oil is normally assessed on 3 parameters: flavor, smell and color. Amongst the variety of olive oils, the extra virgin is the finest with respect to these three parameters.

Olive oil is a mono-unsaturated fatty acid that is rich in antioxidants and is known to promote a longer life while reducing the risk of many lifestyle related diseases. Research proves that the oleic acid in olive oil possesses protective properties that help fight many malignant tumors in the body.

Adding olive oil to your daily cooking can create wonders for you and your family. Unlike other oils used for cooking, olive oil is known to have a suppressing effect on high blood pressure. Diabetics are prescribed a diet rich in olives and olive oil as it has a lower risk of developing obesity. A diet rich in olive oil leads to a healthy and lasting weight loss in comparison to a low-fat diet. Olive oil also boosts the immune system, helps you fight the common infections and keeps you healthy. It is proven to be good for your digestive tract, helps in building stronger bones and improves cognitive function. What more – Olive oil is fantastic for your skin! So if you want to add that extra natural glow on your face, try replacing your regular cooking oil with the versatile olive oil.

Apart from these health benefits, olive oil tastes great! Whether you want to prepare zesty salads, savory soups, scrumptious pastas and risottos or delectable desserts – olive oil is your ingredient! So let's look at the types of olive oil that add this flavor.

Types of Olive Oil:

1. **Extra Virgin Olive Oil:** This is the most expensive olive oil obtained from the first cold-pressing of the fruit. It is

dark green in color and is mostly used in salads and dips as it loses its flavor with high heat while cooking.

2. **Virgin Olive Oil:** This is pale yellow and is also derived from the first cold-press. However, it is slightly more acidic that the extra-virgin oil. This can be used like the extra-virgin variety to give a unique flavor. This oil can be used in pastas where medium heat is required.

3. **Pomace Olive Oil:** This is the refined form of olive oil that is treated with solvents to get rid of the impurities. It is the cheapest form of olive oil available with a bland flavor and is great for all-purpose cooking.

As shared earlier, the flavor of olive oil differs depending on the region. Be it from any country or region, olive oils are ready to use. So let's see some lip-smacking way of including it in your regular cooking.

Chapter 2: 27 Amazing and Easy Everyday Recipes Using Olive oil

With more than a thousand cultivators of olive oil across the world with their unique taste and probably five thousand brands available in the market, finding the right olive for your recipe can be quite a challenge. This chapter will help you overcome this challenge by giving you 27 simple everyday recipes that you can follow and make the family mealtime special. You will find recipes to suit all occasions and you will be surprised as to how a little bit of olive oil can revamp your regular cooking style.

APPETIZERS

1. Eggplants with Mozzarella Cheese

Ingredients:

- 1/4th cup pomace olive oil
- 1 cup fresh basil leaves

- ✓ 3 eggplants, sliced into ½ inch thick discs
- ✓ 1 leek, chopped finely
- ✓ 4 tablespoons white wine vinegar
- ✓ 2 tablespoons olive oil
- ✓ 1 ½ cups mozzarella cheese, shredded
- ✓ Salt to taste

Method: To start with marinate the eggplant slices with salt and set aside for 20-30 minutes.

Basil oil: Blanch the basil leaves for 15-20 seconds in boiling water and drain. Put this in ice cold water for a few seconds and pat the leaves dry with a kitchen towel. Add this to the blender along with olive oil and blend into a puree. Strain the oil.

In a skillet, heat 2 tablespoons of olive oil and on medium heat sauté the leek. Remove and place in a bowl. Add some more oil and cook the eggplants on low heat till they caramelize. Add some vinegar and continue flipping them.

Place the eggplants on a dish and top it with some leek and mozzarella cheese shreds. Sprinkle some basil oil and serve. Add salt and pepper as per taste.

2. Cheesy Broccoli Balls

Ingredients:

For the Balls

- 4 cups broccoli florets
- 1 cup raw almonds, finely ground
- 4 tablespoons pomace olive oil
- $1/4^{th}$ cup parmesan cheese
- $1/4^{th}$ cup fresh basil, finely chopped
- $1/4^{th}$ cup fresh parsley, finely chopped
- 2-3 cloves of garlic, minced
- $1/4^{th}$ teaspoon cayenne pepper

- ✓ 2 large eggs, whisked
- ✓ Salt to taste

For the Sauce

- ✓ 3 tablespoons extra virgin olive oil
- ✓ 1/4th cup white onion, chopped
- ✓ 1 large garlic clove, finely chopped
- ✓ 1 ½ cup of minced tomato

Method: Preheat the oven to 350° F and line the baking tray with a parchment paper. Steam the broccoli till tender. Pulse it till it is finely chopped. To a mixing bowl, add the ground almonds, pulsed broccoli, olive oil, parmesan cheese, basil, parsley, garlic and cayenne pepper. Mix well. Add the whisked eggs and stir well. Shape the mix into small balls and place it in the baking tray and bake for 20-25 minutes or till golden brown.

For the sauce, heat the olive oil on low flame in the skillet and add onion and garlic. Sauté it for a minute. Now stir in the tomato. Cook for a minute and season with salt and pepper. Serve the broccoli balls, hot with the sauce.

3. Bruschetta

Ingredients:

- ✓ 8 Italian bread slices, at least 1/2 inch thick
- ✓ $1/4^{th}$ cup virgin olive oil
- ✓ 3-4 cloves garlic, finely chopped
- ✓ 2 medium tomatoes, thinly sliced
- ✓ 1/2 cup Basil, finely chopped
- ✓ 1/2 tablespoon freshly crushed pepper
- ✓ 1 cup Mozzarella cheese, shredded
- ✓ $1/4^{th}$ cup canned olives, chopped finely

Method: Steep the garlic in warm olive oil for about an hour. Toast bread on a pan until lightly browned on both sides. Rub top of bread with the garlic steeped olive oil. Top this with tomato slices, basil and pepper. Add some shredded mozzarella and chopped green olives and lightly grill on low heat till the cheese melts. Serve hot with tomato ketchup.

4. Olive and Garlic Chicken Nuggets

Ingredients:

- ✓ 3 boneless chicken breasts, cut into bite size chunks

- ✓ 8-10 garlic cloves, chopped and steeped for about an hour in $1/4^{th}$ cup Pomace Olive Oil. Strain and use. (If you love garlic, use as is)

- ✓ ½ tablespoon crushed black pepper

- ✓ ½ cup bread crumbs

- ✓ 1 tablespoon mustard sauce

- ✓ Salt to taste

Method: Marinade chicken in the garlic steeped olive oil, salt and crushed pepper for 30-40 minutes. Drain off excess marinade. Preheat oven to 475° F. Dip both sides of chicken nuggets in the bread crumbs. Arrange the nuggets in a line on a baking sheet and bake for 10 minutes. Flip the nuggets and bake for 5 more minutes till light brown. Serve warm with mustard sauce.

5. Smoked Salmon in Tartare

Ingredients:

- ✓ 2 cups smoked salmon, diced into small pieces
- ✓ 1/4th cup red onions, diced finely
- ✓ 1/4th cup capers
- ✓ 1/4th cup extra virgin olive oil
- ✓ Juice from 1 fresh lemon
- ✓ 1 tablespoon freshly ground pepper

- ✓ 1/2 cup sour cream
- ✓ 8 tsp fresh dill leaves, finely chopped
- ✓ 3-4 Crackers
- ✓ Some kosher salt to taste

Method: In a mixing bowl combine salmon, onions, capers, olive oil and lemon juice & mix. Season this mixture with freshly ground pepper and kosher salt. Combine sour cream, dill and some salt in a separate bowl & mix well. Top each cracker with the salmon-tartare mix & small dollop of dill sour cream mixture.

6. Corn and Olive Salsa

Ingredients:

- ✓ 2 cups American corn, grilled
- ✓ 1 cup canned black beans, drain well
- ✓ 2 cups tomatoes, finely diced

- ✓ 1/2 red onion, finely chopped
- ✓ 3/4th cup fresh cilantro leaves, finely chopped
- ✓ 1/2 lime, freshly squeezed
- ✓ 4 tablespoons jalapeno balsamic vinegar
- ✓ Salt to taste

Method: Combine the corn, beans, tomatoes, red onion and cilantro in a large mixing bowl. Mix well. Stir in some lime juice, balsamic vinegar and salt. Refrigerate for about 3 hours to allow the juices to blend. Serve chilled with nachos or tortilla chips

SOUPS

1. Roasted Butternut Squash Soup

Ingredients:

- ✓ 3 cups butternut squash, diced

- ✓ 1/4th cup virgin olive oil and extra for brushing
- ✓ A handful of sage, chopped and steeped in the above olive oil
- ✓ 1 tablespoon butter
- ✓ 1 medium onion, chopped
- ✓ ½ teaspoon kosher salt
- ✓ ½ teaspoon freshly ground pepper
- ✓ 3 tablespoons brandy
- ✓ 1 ½ cup chicken broth
- ✓ Pinch of nutmeg powder
- ✓ 3/4th cup fresh cream, whipped

Method: Preheat oven to 375° F. Brush the butternut squash pieces with virgin olive oil and place in a roasting pan and roast in the oven for about 45 minutes till soft. Remove and cool.

On medium heat, add 1/4th cup of sage steeped olive oil with butter. Add onion and cook till translucent. Sprinkle with salt and pepper and stir well. Add the brandy and let it evaporate.

Scoop out the cooked squash, add the cooked onion and the remaining ingredients and blend well in a blender. Pour this into a pan and bring to boil. Add the whipped cream and stir well. Serve piping hot with soup sticks.

2. Nutty Sweet Potato Soup

Ingredients:

- ✓ 2 large sweet potatoes, cooked, peeled and diced
- ✓ 1/4th cup extra virgin olive oil
- ✓ 1/4th cup tomato sauce
- ✓ 2-3 tablespoons almond milk (you can also use normal milk)
- ✓ 4 cups water

- ✓ ½ cup cashew nuts, coarsely chopped
- ✓ ½ teaspoon dried thyme
- ✓ Kosher salt and ground black pepper to taste

Method: Mash the sweet potatoes in a bowl. Place these mashed potatoes in a skillet on a medium flame. Stir in the extra virgin olive oil, tomato sauce, water and almond milk. Stir well till all the mashed sweet potato blends well with other ingredients. Now add salt, pepper, thyme and the cashew nuts and mix it well. Bring the mixture to a boil and turn off the heat. Cool this and puree well in a blender. Serve hot and garnish with a tablespoon of olive oil and some dried thyme.

3. Cauliflower Soup

Ingredients:

- ✓ 1 cup florets of cauliflower

- ✓ 5 tablespoons of extra virgin olive oil
- ✓ 2 medium onions, thinly sliced
- ✓ 2 garlic cloves, minced
- ✓ ½ teaspoon coriander powder
- ✓ ½ teaspoon turmeric powder
- ✓ 1 teaspoon cumin
- ✓ 1 cup coconut milk
- ✓ 3 ½ cups water
- ✓ Salt and pepper to taste

Method: Heat olive oil on low flame and sauté onions with some salt till translucent. Stir in garlic and sauté for another minute. Now add all the remaining ingredients except the coconut milk. Bring the soup to boil till the cauliflower turns tender. Cool and puree in a blender. Pour the pureed soup back to the pan and add coconut milk. Stir well and add salt and pepper to taste. Serve hot.

4. Greek Lemon and Chicken Soup

Ingredients:

- ✓ 6 cups fresh chicken broth
- ✓ 1/2 cup orzo (Available at any grocery shop)
- ✓ 6 egg yolks, beaten well
- ✓ 1 1/2 cups rotisserie chicken, shredded
- ✓ 1/4 cup fresh lemon juice
- ✓ Kosher salt and black pepper to taste

Method: Bring the chicken stock to a boil in a large saucepan. Add the orzo and boil for about 10-15 minutes till tender. In a large bowl, add the beaten egg yolks and slowly drizzle 1 cup of the hot stock while whisking it vigorously. Add the egg mixture to a saucepan, and continue whisking occasionally, until it gets thickened to the consistency of heavy cream. This might take some time, but be patient. Stir in the lemon juice and continue stirring. Add the shredded chicken and cook for another minute.

Season this with salt and pepper as per taste and serve hot.

5. Mexican Seafood Soup

Ingredients:

- ✓ 1 tablespoon pomace olive oil
- ✓ 1 cup onion, finely chopped
- ✓ 3 garlic cloves, minced
- ✓ 3 cups canned clam broth
- ✓ 1/2 cup orzo (Available at any grocery shop)
- ✓ 1 cup pureed tomato
- ✓ 2 tablespoons of sun dried tomato in oil
- ✓ 1 tablespoon lemon rind, grated
- ✓ 1 cup seafood mix – shrimps, squids, scallops (or as desired)
- ✓ 4 tablespoons of fresh cilantro, finely chopped

Method: Heat olive oil in large skillet over medium heat and add the chopped onion. Sauté this well until tender and translucent. Add the minced garlic and keep stirring. Add the clam broth and the next 4 ingredients and stir well. Simmer for 5-10 minutes. Keep aside for about an hour to let the juice blend well. Now add the seafood mix as desired and simmer along with some chopped cilantro. Add salt and pepper as required. Serve hot in bowls and garnish with fresh cilantro.

SALADS

1. Bow tie Pasta Salad

Ingredients:

- ✓ 1 cup Bowtie pasta, boiled and drained
- ✓ 2 cups fresh spinach, finely chopped and blanched
- ✓ $1/3^{rd}$ cup feta cheese, crumbled
- ✓ $1/4^{th}$ cup red onion, finely chopped

- ✓ 1 cup cherry tomatoes, halved
- ✓ 1/2 teaspoon basil, dried and crumbled
- ✓ 1/4th cup extra virgin olive oil
- ✓ 1/4th cup balsamic vinegar
- ✓ Salt to taste

Method: Transfer the bowtie pasta to a large bowl and stir in the blanched spinach, crumbled feta, chopped onion, tomatoes and basil. Toss with extra virgin olive oil and balsamic vinegar. Add salt as per taste. Refrigerate and serve cold.

2. Pear and Blue Cheese Salad

Ingredients:

- ✓ 1 lettuce, torn into bite-size chunks
- ✓ 3 Pears, cored and chopped
- ✓ ½ cup blue cheese, crumbled

- ✓ 1 avocado, diced
- ✓ ½ cup spring onions, thinly sliced
- ✓ 1/4th cup white sugar + 1 tablespoon for dressing
- ✓ ½ cup pecans
- ✓ 1/3rd cup extra virgin olive oil
- ✓ 3 tablespoons red wine vinegar
- ✓ 2 tablespoons honey and garlic mustard sauce
- ✓ 3 cloves garlic, chopped
- ✓ ½ tablespoon salt
- ✓ Black pepper, freshly ground

Method: Place a skillet on medium heat. Add 1/4th cup sugar together with the pecans. Keep stirring till the sugar melts and caramelizes the pecans. Now transfer them on butter paper and allow cooling. Break it into pieces.

For Dressing: Mix oil, vinegar, sugar, mustard sauce, chopped garlic, salt and pepper in a bowl. In a large bowl, layer the lettuce pieces, pears, crumbled blue cheese, diced avocado and the spring onions. Now pour the dressing and sprinkle some caramelized pecans.

3. Quinoa Salad

Ingredients:

- 3 cups quinoa, cooked
- 4 tablespoons extra virgin olive oil
- 4 tablespoons balsamic vinegar
- Kosher Salt to taste
- $1/3^{rd}$ cup cucumber, finely diced
- $1/3^{rd}$ cup tomatoes, finely diced
- $1/3^{rd}$ cup green olives, diced into halves

Method: Place the first 4 ingredients in a salad bowl and mix well. In the end add the balance ingredients and give it a gentle stir. Refrigerate and serve cool with grilled fish, chicken or lamb.

4. Summer Salad

Ingredients:

- ✓ 2 cucumbers, thinly sliced
- ✓ 4 tomatoes, cut into 8-10 wedges
- ✓ 2 sweet onions, thinly sliced
- ✓ 1/4th cup extra virgin olive oil
- ✓ 3 tablespoons balsamic vinegar
- ✓ ½ tablespoon freshly ground black pepper
- ✓ Salt to taste

Method: Place the cucumbers, tomatoes and onions in a bowl and pour in the remaining ingredients. Mix well and serve chilled.

5. Chicken and Avocado Salad

Ingredients:

- 1 cup cherry tomatoes, halved
- 1/4th cup red onion, chopped coarsely
- ½ cup orange, peeled and deseeded
- ½ cup strawberries, chopped
- 2 avocados, diced
- ½ cup chicken, boiled and shredded
- 1 tablespoon balsamic vinegar
- 1 tablespoon extra virgin olive oil
- 1/4th cup fresh cilantro, chopped
- Pinch Sea salt and ground pepper

Method: Combine all the ingredients in a bowl (except avocado). Mix well. Now add the avocado and toss gently. Season with salt and pepper and serve cold.

6. Festive Salad

Ingredients:

- 8 cups baby spinach, chopped coarsely
- 1/2 red onion, sliced into rings
- 1 can (about 1 cup) mandarin oranges, drained
- 1/2 cup cranberries, dried (not candied)
- 1 cup honey roasted nuts and dry fruits, coarsely chopped (you can choose from almonds, pecans, raisins or walnuts
- 1 cup feta cheese, crumbled
- 1/2 cup extra virgin olive oil
- 1/2 cup balsamic vinegar

Method: Place the spinach on the salad plates as a base layer. Toss the other ingredients in a separate bowl and chill for about an hour. Top the spinach with the salad mix. You can garnish with some more extra virgin olive oil as per your taste.

PASTA AND RICE

1. Courgette Rice with Olives

Ingredients:

- ✓ 100 g feta cheese, crumbled
- ✓ ½ cup black pitted olives, roughly chopped
- ✓ A handful of fresh parsley, finely chopped
- ✓ 6 tablespoon virgin olive oil
- ✓ 1 large onion, finely chopped
- ✓ 2 courgettes, roughly chopped
- ✓ ½ cup green peas
- ✓ 250 g risotto rice
- ✓ 1 litre vegetable stock

Method: In a mixing bowl, combine the feta, olives, parsley and 2 tablespoons of olive oil. Mix well. Add the remaining olive oil in a skillet and heat. Add the onions and sizzle for 4-5 minutes. Add the courgettes and stir till half cooked. Now stir in the rice and the vegetable stock. Heat till all the water is absorbed and the rice cooks. Add the peas and stir well till rice turns sticky and creamy. Now mix in the feta mix and stir. Serve hot.

2. Orange and Caper Pasta

Ingredients:

- ✓ 1/2 cup virgin olive oil
- ✓ 2 large onions, finely sliced
- ✓ 4 tablespoons orange zest, grated
- ✓ 2 garlic cloves, minced
- ✓ 1 cup chicken broth
- ✓ 1 cup penne pasta, cooked and drained
- ✓ 2 tablespoons capers, drained
- ✓ $1/4^{th}$ cup fresh parsley leaves, minced

- ✓ Sea salt and freshly ground black pepper to taste

Method: In a large saucepan, heat the olive oil over medium heat and sauté the onions until translucent. Add the orange zest and garlic and cook for about 2 minutes. Reduce the heat to low and pour in the chicken stock. Simmer for 10 minutes. Now toss in the boiled penne and mix well. Add the capers, parsley, salt and pepper. This serves as a tasty as a main course that complements grilled seafood or chicken.

3. Lime Shrimp with Cilantro Rice

Ingredients:

- ✓ ½ cup shrimps, raw, skinned and deveined
- ✓ ½ cup + 2 tablespoons virgin olive oil, divided
- ✓ ½ tablespoon citrus seasoning blend
- ✓ 1 cup jasmine rice, cooked and drained

- ✓ 2 tablespoon fresh cilantro leaves, chopped
- ✓ Sea salt to taste

Method: In a small bowl, mix 1/4th cup olive oil and the citrus seasoning blend. Mix this marinade with the shrimps and seal it in a Ziploc bag for 30 minutes. Heat 2 tablespoons olive oil in a large sauté pan on medium heat and cook the shrimp for about 2-3 minutes each side.

Mix the jasmine rice, cilantro, 1/4th cup olive oil and sea salt in a large bowl. Serve it steaming hot by topping it with the shrimps.

4. Balsamic Chicken with Jasmine Rice

Ingredients:

- ✓ 6 boneless chicken breasts, whole
- ✓ 3 cups tomatoes OR 2 cans of herbed tomatoes

- ✓ 1 cup artichoke hearts, drained
- ✓ 1 medium onion, thinly sliced
- ✓ 5-6 garlic cloves, peeled and whole
- ✓ ½ cup balsamic vinegar
- ✓ ½ cup extra virgin olive oil
- ✓ 1 tablespoon dried oregano
- ✓ 1 tablespoon dried Basil
- ✓ 1 tablespoon dried Rosemary
- ✓ ½ tablespoon dried Thyme
- ✓ Freshly ground black pepper and sea salt to taste
- ✓ 2 cups jasmine rice, cooked

Method: Pour the olive oil in a heavy bottom pan and add the chicken breasts. Sprinkle some salt and pepper each breast. Add a layer of sliced onion on top of chicken and then add all the dried herbs and garlic cloves. Lastly sprinkle vinegar and top it all with tomatoes and artichokes. Cook on high 2 hours on medium flame while checking on the chicken. Serve with jasmine rice. If you cook on low for a longer time, you can also add in ½ cup of chicken broth so as to avoid charring.

5. Roasted Cauliflower with Brown Rice

Ingredients:

- 6 cups cauliflower florets
- $1/4^{th}$ cup extra virgin olive oil
- 1 tablespoon garlic, finely sliced
- 2 tablespoons fresh lemon juice
- 1 tablespoon sea salt
- ½ tablespoon black pepper, freshly ground
- 2 tablespoons parmesan cheese, crumbled
- 2 tablespoons fresh chives, coarsely chopped
- 2 cups brown rice, cooked

Method: Preheat oven to 450°F. Place the cauliflower florets in a baking dish. Sprinkle some olive oil over the cauliflower, and flavor it with some garlic, lemon juice, salt and pepper. Place the pan in the pre-heated oven and cook for about 10-15 minutes. Keep stirring it sporadically. Once done, remove from the oven and sprinkle some crumbled parmesan cheese. Mix well and garnish with chives. Let the juices seep and you can serve it hot with some brown rice.

6. Cheesy Greek Macaroni

Ingredients:

- ✓ 1 cup macaroni, cooked and drained (sprinkle some olive oil to avoid sticking and enhance flavor)

- ✓ 6 cups feta cheese, crumbled

- ✓ 2 ½ cups toned milk

- ✓ 2 tablespoons lemon juice, fresh

- ✓ 2/3rd cup virgin olive oil

- ✓ 1 tablespoon kosher salt
- ✓ 2 tablespoons black pepper, fresh ground
- ✓ 1 tablespoon fresh rosemary leaves, minced
- ✓ 2 tablespoons fresh thyme, minced
- ✓ 1 tablespoon garlic, minced
- ✓ 1/2 tablespoon paprika flakes
- ✓ ½ cup cherry tomatoes, halved
- ✓ ½ cup parmesan cheese, grated

Method: Preheat oven to 350°F. Add feta cheese, milk, lemon juice, olive oil, salt, and pepper to a blender and blend well. This mixture will not be entirely smooth. You will see some small chunks of cheese. Add this cheese mix to the cooked macaroni and stir well. Now add chopped herbs and spices - rosemary, thyme, garlic, red pepper flakes and finally the tomatoes. Pour this mixture into a rectangular baking dish and generously sprinkle parmesan cheese on the top. Bake for about 20 minutes till the cheese is browned. Serve hot.

7. Brown Rice with Broccoli

Ingredients:

- ½ cup brown rice, half-cooked and strained
- 1/4th cup water
- 5 tablespoons virgin olive oil
- ½ cup broccoli florets
- 4 garlic cloves, chopped
- 1 tablespoon fresh cumin, roasted and ground
- ½ cup boneless chicken, boiled and shredded
- Salt and pepper to taste

Method: Take olive oil in a pan and stir fry the garlic, cumin, broccoli and chicken. Add salt and pepper as per choice. Now add the brown rice and stir well. Add some water and cover it for about 5 minutes till the half-cooked brown rice gets cooked and the water evaporates. Serve hot with grilled seafood or chicken.

DESSERTS

1. Baked Apple Crisp

Ingredients:

- ✓ 4 cups apples, peeled and thinly sliced
- ✓ ½ cup brown sugar
- ✓ 2 tablespoons fresh lemon juice
- ✓ 1 cup all-purpose flour
- ✓ 3/4th cup granulated sugar
- ✓ 1 tablespoon baking powder
- ✓ ½ tablespoon salt
- ✓ 1 egg, lightly beaten
- ✓ 1/4th cup virgin olive oil
- ✓ 4 tablespoons butter, melted

- ✓ ½ tablespoon Cinnamon powder
- ✓ Red Apple balsamic vinegar for drizzling

Method: Preheat oven to 350°F. In a baking dish, add the apple slices, brown sugar and lemon juice. Mix and spread in a layer. In a separate bowl, mix flour, granulated sugar, baking powder and salt together. Add the beaten egg and mix until the mixture turns crumbly. Now spread this crumbled mix on the apples evenly. Pour olive oil and butter and sprinkle cinnamon powder on the top. Bake for about 25-30 minutes. Spray some red apple balsamic vinegar and serve hot with some vanilla ice cream.

2. Orange and Almond Brownies

Ingredients:

- ✓ ½ cup dark chocolate
- ✓ 10 tablespoons pomace olive oil

- ✓ ½ cup orange rinds
- ✓ 4 eggs, beaten lightly
- ✓ 3/4th cup ground almonds
- ✓ 1 cup granulated sugar
- ✓ 1 teaspoon baking soda
- ✓ ½ cup all purpose flour

Method: Preheat the oven to 350°F. Grease an 8×10-inch baking dish with some olive oil or butter and keep aside.

Steep the orange rinds in the olive oil (slightly warm it) and leave for about an hour, so that the orange flavor blends with the olive oil. You can either strain the rinds out or leave it as is. This is your orange flavored olive oil.

Break the dark chocolate into smaller chunks and keep in a double boiler till it melts into a smooth liquid. Stir in the orange olive oil and mix well. Now remove the chocolate from heat and let it cool. In a separate mixing bowl, combine the beaten eggs, ground almonds and sugar and mix well. To this add the melted chocolate mix and stir well. In another bowl, sift together the baking soda and flour and mix this with the chocolate mixture. Stir well to blend. Pour this batter in the greased baking dish and bake for about 25 minutes. Cool and store in an airtight jar.

3. Olive and Lemon Custard

Ingredients:

- ✓ 3 eggs

- ✓ ½ cup granulated sugar

- ✓ ½ cup fresh lemon juice

- ✓ 2 tablespoons of lemon zest, devoid the pith

- ✓ ½ teaspoon vanilla essence

- ✓ ½ cup extra virgin olive oil

Method: Place all ingredients (except olive oil) in a high speed blender and blend well for at least 4-5 minutes. Pour in the olive oil and continue the high speed blending till you see the custard firming up. Pour this mix into a double boiler and keep stirring till the mixture thickens further (this means the eggs are cooked). This might take about 3-4 minutes. Refrigerate and serve chilled.

Chapter 3: Your Shopping List - Essential Ingredients used in this Book

Enlisted below is a list of ingredients you will come across in this book. Make sure you have them all stocked up in your kitchen.

- ✓ **Olive Oils** – Extra virgin, Virgin, Pomace
- ✓ **Cheese:** Mozzarella, Parmesan, Feta, Blue cheese
- ✓ **Honey glazed nuts** – Almonds, walnuts, pecans
- ✓ **Common Herbs** – Basil, Parsley, Cilantro, Dill, Sage, Thyme, Rosemary,
- ✓ **Common Spices** – Pepper, Nutmeg, Paprika, Cayenne pepper, Cinnamon
- ✓ **Vinegar** – Red wine vinegar, White wine vinegar, Balsamic vinegar, Red Apple balsamic vinegar

- ✓ **Broths** – Vegetable, Chicken, Seafood
- ✓ **Tinned food** – Black beans, mandarin oranges, tomatoes
- ✓ **Sauces and Blends** – Mustard sauce, Honey and garlic mustard sauce, Citrus Seasoning blend
- ✓ **Rice** – Risotto, Jasmine, Brown, White
- ✓ **Olives** – Black and Green Pitted
- ✓ **Pasta** – Penne, Bowtie, Fusilli, Macaroni
- ✓ **Sugar** – Granulated, Brown
- ✓ **Baking related** – baking soda, all-purpose flour
- ✓ Capers
- ✓ Crackers
- ✓ Sour cream
- ✓ Kosher Salt
- ✓ Almond milk
- ✓ Orzo
- ✓ Artichoke hearts

- ✓ Quinoa
- ✓ Vanilla Essence

Conclusion

Thank you again for purchasing this book!

I hope this book was able to give you enough information on the goodness of olive oil and how you can include it in your day-to-day cooking. I am sure I have motivated you to replace your regular oil with olive oil.

Now that you are aware of various health benefits that it has to offer, the different types of olive oil mentioned in this book should be number one on your shopping list. Start with a few regular dishes like a stir fry or a salad and see how adding a little bit of this oil can work wonders for you! It won't take you long to realize that this 'liquid gold' is great for you and the health of your family. I didn't see any visible challenge in adapting to this oil in my daily cooking; hence I can confidently assure you that you too can do it! Olive oil easily adapts and blends with the local flavors of indigenous herbs and spices to give you a unique culinary experience. This sort of adaptation is unheard of.

With lifestyle related diseases like atherosclerosis, congestive heart diseases, diabetes, hypertension and obesity, on the rise, the urgent need is to brace yourself up for a healthy life. By using olive oil in your daily cooking, I firmly believe you can look forward to a long, active and healthy life. So go ahead, try the recipes shared here and add in a bit of your creativity too!

Finally, if you enjoyed this book, please take the time to share your thoughts and post a review on Amazon. It'd be greatly appreciated!

Thank you and good luck!

Printed in Great Britain
by Amazon